20 Life Lessons To Find
Real Happiness

Pursuing
Happiness

Farima Wassel Joya

7reasures
PRESS

Copyright © 2018

Printed in the United States

20 Life Lesson Series – Vol. 4
Pursuing Happiness
20 Life Lessons to Find Real Happiness
First Edition

By: Farima Wassel Joya
www.farimajoya.com

Published by 7 Treasures Press

ISBN-13: 978-0-9986611-8-6 (7 Treasures Press)
ISBN-10: 0-9986611-8-X

Library of Congress Control Number: 2018913211

www.7treasures.com
7tpress@7treasures.com
(510) 275-3497

10 9 8 7 6 5 4 3 2 1

To my beloved mother, Nasrin Wassel

Introduction:

Life is a journey, not a destination. A happy life is about moving from one moment to the next with contentment, even if the moment is perceived to be negative. Happy people seem to have control of their state of mind in negative situations. It is about how they view and deal with daily challenges without being affected physically or emotionally. They are focused, and they seem to be calm and make better decisions. Happy people enjoy long-lasting, rewarding relationships; they tend to be healthier and end up living longer. Who wouldn't want that?

I have been fascinated with the idea of achieving happiness since I was a child. I saw how hard my father was working, for so many hours, and he was away from home and his family. I was thirsty for spending some time with him, but he would always say, "I have to work." From that time on, my relationship with money was never developed and it never became a motivating factor in my life. In my adult life, I never compared myself with anyone and never felt bad because of my lifestyle. I was not rich, but I was not poor either. I had more than enough to be thankful for every day of my life. I was not involved in any race to make more, do more and have more. My goal was to create happy childhood experiences for my children and make it a happy life as much as possible. Luckily, my husband's relationship with money was even worse than mine. He spends as if there's no tomorrow, and I love that about him. I'm glad that we gave happiness a priority in our life. Of course, it has gotten us close to trouble so many times, but we have been able to find creative ways to get us out of those situations. Somehow, we always find our way.

Achieving happiness from within is more spiritual than emotional. The goal is to access the happy place within you to display emotional happiness around you. To reach that blissful state of mind and way of living, we must dig a little deeper within ourselves and find it. All we need to do is to take an inward journey that requires awareness, time, and effort.

In this book, I'm trying to help you understand that experiencing happiness, true happiness, inner peace, bliss or joy is not only for the enlightened individuals or practicing yogis. Ordinary people also can approach life from a spiritual angle to find true joy without a deep dive into understanding consciousness. It is not necessary to have a deep understanding or ask why and how questions; it is enough to take the words of wise teachers and accept them.

I hope no one leaves this world without experiencing their inner joy and bliss in both positive and negative situations of life. This inner joy makes it clear what is important in life and what is not. The sad news is that many will not pursue true happiness readily because it's not available for purchase with one click of a mouse. Some only become aware of the need for inner peace and personal contentment when they experience a great loss, whether it's their health, their relationships, their loved ones or their financial empire. And, sadly some people will never experience bliss in their life.

Happiness is a state of mind that exists in each one of us no matter if we use it or not. It might be buried under layers of protective shields that we have built around it. We don't know much about our spirituality because it has not been part of our normal education system. Especially in the West, we have to find it the hard way. The East, or in the old ancient civilizations of the Greeks, Indians, Chinese and Persians, philosophy is imbedded with poetry, religion, literature and lifestyle, and is well rooted into each household. I remember analyzing

Khayyam, Hafiz and Firdausi's poetry in grade school. Although our maturity was not fully developed enough to understand it, we were exposed to the spiritual side of life through great stories of compassion, suffering, emptiness, greatness, love and respect.

Our society's desire today is to move forward, and in both the East and West it has been focused on commercialism and advancement in technology. We think that we can solve our outer life challenges from outside sources, not knowing that we are moving away from our biological sense of being and solving all our challenges from inside out.

Today, we believe what we see, and we see what we believe. We are so preoccupied with things and events in our life that we don't have time to ask deep questions about life, the meaning of life, why we do what we do, and the reasons for our existence. To understand the deep philosophies of life, we must dedicate time and energy into practicing enlightenment, and that is not something that can be achieved overnight. Certainly, it is not on everyone's agenda to become a practicing spiritual person to find the happiness within.

There are some spiritual teachers who practice hours upon hours, sitting in silent meditation with closed eyes and living in remote places, who have achieved mastery of physical matters in the world of consciousness, but what good does it do for the rest of humanity? We know these people exist, and we know that enlightenment is possible, and they have been around for centuries. All the world's religions have some sort of self-mastery phenomenon, and a dedicated group of followers who claim to have achieved enlightenment. This is not a new practice or knowledge.

To become a practicing spiritual person is one thing, but to put the practices of spirituality to use in our everyday life is something else. To use the benefits of spirituality in our daily life, it is enough to be aware of it and know how to use spiritual teachings without feeling overwhelmed or doing weird things that you are not used to. Just as it is enough to understand the basics of physics, chemistry, geography or history, it is enough to know that we are spiritual beings consisting of a body, a mind and a spirit. The goal of spirituality is to recognize that there's a power beyond our understanding that protects life and is in constant change. To understand this fact, it is possible, even

5

for critics, to reflect and take a few spirituality lessons to live by.

Why Happiness?

Happiness is our true nature. Just like any other element in our environment, we have a life cycle and our existence, compared to the billions of years of the Earth's age, doesn't even amount to the size of a speck of dust. What could be the purpose of our existence? We probably can better answer this question if we ask, what is the purpose of a tree, or a mountain, or a tiger, or a bee? We all are created to Be and to serve to our capacity. The one obstacle that has added to human misery is the value that we have given our thoughts. We think we can solve our daily problems and challenges with our knowledge, but the further we go to ignore our consciousness or the soul, the unhappier we get.

The Latin philosopher René Descartes said in the mid-sixteenth century, "I think, therefore I am." With this philosophy, humans have since achieved great advancements, but the fundamental purpose of existence has still not been identified.

Now, we put the pieces of the puzzle back together and find that we are not a "drop in the ocean, but an ocean in a drop," as Rumi said more than 800 years ago.

We can choose to live as a drop or as the ocean. A drop's view is small, insignificant, vulnerable and limited, but the ocean's view is vast, abundant, powerful and unlimited. We can run around like a drop looking for the ocean, while we are an ocean if we stay still and focus on who we really are. That's all we need to know.

Happiness is a choice that we make in the present moment. It's our emotional response to our current situation. Whether we are experiencing a positive or negative situation right now, at this second, it's how we interpret and how we respond to that situation that makes us happy or unhappy. Besides that, if we look at the issue from a practical side, like I do, there are things we can do to put luck on our side and make life as enjoyable as possible for ourselves and our loved ones around us.

Life can be lived in a much simpler way than we are living now, and this book outlines twenty life lessons to experience a blissful life, whether we choose to practice higher spirituality or not. These are life lessons that no one will tell us readily, and if we simply take the time to come to it naturally, it

7

will cost us time, money, energy, our family, our happiness and maybe our health.

We have a list of twenty life lessons that make us think and might inspire us to stop taking life so seriously and to experience the true joy and inner peace that is already within us. Again, our happiness is not dependent on any outside sources; rather, it is our inner response to our current situations. Change that, and we'll live life as practicing enlightened mystics in regular outfits.

Sharing Is Caring!

Dedicated to my dear and kind mother, Nasrin Wassel, who often experienced the worst side of life since childhood and carries an enormous amount of negative emotions and hurt feelings to this day. Perhaps this is one of the reasons why I was fascinated with the subject of inner peace and true happiness. My love for her is real and unconditional.

Share this spiritual gift with people you care about.

1

ALIGN OUR BODY, MIND AND SOUL

If there's any reason for us not to be happy in our life, it is because we want one thing but do something else. This can be true in our personal lives, relationships and at work. It simply means that our outer image and identity is in opposition with our inner identity. We experience the feelings of being unsatisfied, frustrated or even disappointed at our choices regardless of how our life has turned out to be as grownups.

As children, we had a clear image of what a perfect life would be when we grow up. We knew what we were going to do, who to marry, and how many children we would have, but somehow, we forgot those images by the time we filled out that job application, or said "I do," or mistakenly took the wrong route. Very soon we realize that this person we've married is not the person we dreamed about, and this job is not what we wanted to do. It's at this time that our core reality and desires have traveled far away from what we imagined in our childhood fantasies.

However, it is never too late to change course and to align our body, mind and spirit once again as adults and learn to live an authentic life as we are. Gandhi said, "When what we think with what we say and what we do are in harmony, that is happiness." This simply means that we don't play drama or life games with ourselves and others to make a living, but we are courageous enough to be ourselves and live with ease.

If we are not living our authentic life, it means that we are either not clear on our true inner desires or we are filling a role that is expected of us by our parents, spouse, children, and others. However, soon we realize that only we are responsible for accomplishing our life's goals, mission, purpose, vision and outcome. While others might want to see us happy and successful, they honestly don't know what makes us happy, so they project their own perception of a happy life on their loved ones.

To align our body, mind and spirit is to bring some changes to our lifestyle. Whether we change it slowly or abruptly is up to us, but the sooner we decide to be our authentic self from inside out, the sooner we'll see a real change. It might alienate and frustrate some our closest relationships for a short time, but it'll make us happier from within. With this newfound spirituality, we will build fulfilling relationships, higher income and better health.

Before I began to explore spirituality, I always solved my problems with logic, reasoning and experience. What was missing in my life was the connection to my soul. I'd accomplished everything I wanted, and had a kind and supportive husband, wonderful kids, good jobs and business, awesome extended family and community, living in the best area of the best state and the best country, but I still felt something was missing. I thought to myself that my happiness is out there, and I will find it one day, but when that day would come, I didn't know.

I knew that something like a soul existed but never had the understanding to search and find it within me. I learned from numerous teachers, books, and courses that I could discover my inner world with meditation. I was actively in search of inner peace and higher spirituality. After practicing meditation for two years, I made the connection with my soul, and once I made the connection, I was not the same person I was before. In the beginning, my

11

practical mind didn't know how to analyze this wonderful experience, how to describe it and how to use it. Naturally, I became a carefree, kind, humble, generous, fearless and vulnerable person. I could see everything more clearly and could make better and faster decisions.

As a result, I know who I am and what I want and what is my purpose. Now, I understand that happiness is not out there, but it is in small things happening around me. It is how I perceive and interpret small and large events in my life today. I feel present; I enjoy the moment and I am ready to live my life journey in the unknown territory. I feel as one divine soul that is eternally grateful to be alive and experience life the way I do so far, and for every other day that I continue to live. With my authentic self in mind, it's my goal to be honest first with myself and then with others.

I'm actively listening to how my heart guides me with the anticipation of living a purposeful life. I'm sure that slowly it will become a daily habit. To forget about the world, small stresses of daily life, and other people's problems and focus on how I could be a better human being is not an easy task, but it's the most long-lasting, rewarding thing we can do for ourselves that makes this life worth living.

There's no right or wrong way that we should align ourselves with our true nature. Only we know our own true nature. If it feels right at the time, that is the right thing to do, say or think. The moment we feel discomfort and uneasiness is the moment that we are no longer our authentic self and should correct our alignment. At that time, we should ask ourselves where this uneasiness comes from— whether it is real fear or imaginary; whether it's our own limiting beliefs, ego, or other people's judgement about us. Once we've acknowledged the cause of the discomfort, we can consciously make a decision to live with it for the rest of our lives.

We need to allow ourselves to make mistakes, and then once we realize that mistake, own it and go a step further and apologize if we hurt anyone unintentionally. It's okay to admit our mistakes and wrongdoings, but it's not okay to live with the guilt for any length of time. If anything from the past is still unresolved in our mind, we can either fix it if it's possible or forget it forever. I've never allowed myself to make mistakes and have preferred to use my mind versus my heart to lead my life. Now that I have found that my heart represents my soul, I'd much rather use my heart than my mind to make my decisions.

Our body is autonomous. It works with or without our intentions, but it depends on how we take care of it physically. What we eat, how much rest we take, how active we are, what is our energy level, and how deep and fast we fall asleep at night. What is our body's capacity? It is wonderful to understand our body's capacity and listen to ourselves internally. To know how our lungs need to breathe better, what our heart needs to pump better, and what our kidneys need to work better. If we meditate and try to listen to each organ of our body, we can understand what each one of our organs wants from us. This is how we can heal ourselves from injuries and disease that we might be experiencing. However, at the beginning of our spiritual journey, it is enough to understand that our body needs healthy food, enough rest, and daily movement to function properly.

In its natural state, the body is full of energy and excitement with no pain in its authentic state. How long we can maintain our body at an optimum level depends on our involvement and the responsibility we take for how we treat our body from this moment on.

When we are connected to the center of our heart's desire or our soul and enjoy our optimal body with energy and zest for living, our mind very seldom wanders to negative territory. Even if it does occasionally experience fear, self-doubt, judgement, jealousy, greed or any other negative emotional thought patterns, these lasts for a very short time. Once we recognize that we have the negative thought or feeling, we can correct it immediately. The dialog in our mind never stops, but it can be consciously controlled until it becomes a habit and autonomous.

2

SERVE FROM OUR SOUL

I spent three nights in the hospital when my daughter was giving birth. There were several nurses who came and worked their shift and left for the day. Among all, there was one nurse who not only was doing her job, but she genuinely cared for her patient. The energy, support and feeling that she gave us was beyond her call of duty. I realized that she did her job from a position of compassion, support, kindness and humbleness without any expectations back from us or anyone else. This is an example of how we serve from our soul with what we do.

Unless we perform from a position of passion and compassion, we'll feel the emptiness. When we go to work, we are expected to do a set of chores that promotes the service and products that our company is built for. Most of us don't enjoy what we do for living because it feels like a job we must do. We don't enjoy the people we work with, we

16

don't get enough rewards or appreciation for what we do, or we work for a boss that we don't get along with. The moment the idea of doing something else for a living than what we currently do enters our mind, it will be downhill from there.

Most of us don't choose what we do for a living because we get the first job that will pay our bills and we get stuck with that job. However, before changing our mind about our job and what we do, there's a better way to make our work enjoyable.

First, if we are happy within ourselves and how our life is going, we will not let anything disturb our state of being in any situation. Second, if we are a happy and proactive person, we will look at every challenge as an opportunity and a chance to try to solve problems instead of creating or enlarging them.

A better way to make our job enjoyable and turn it into something that we can look forward to is to see the real benefit that we are offering our customers and clients. How do our services and products change their lives? Once we know that we are a team member in creating that change, we'll overlook the small negative details or our differences with our coworkers and continue to make a difference the best way we can.

Blissed individuals look at people problems differently than average. They see and feel people when they are in a rush or have stress as being afraid. They view the actions of other people as innocent cries for help, so they can either offer help or understand that people behave according to how their life is going for them. Mostly people are too deep into their own problems that they don't realize what effects their actions create.

This is how we can make our job an opportunity to serve in any capacity we have. We take responsibility for our own inner happiness and satisfaction with what we do, ignoring all the negative things that are out of our control. If we are doctors and the real reason why we became doctors in the first place was to help sick people, then that should be the focus of our work, not behind-the-job bureaucracies. If we are a teacher, if we are a firefighter, if we are a policeman, if we are a flight attendant, if we are a mechanic, if we are a bus driver, if we are a business owner, or if we are an artist, we can find the passion and compassion to serve from our soul and live a happy life from inside out.

After years of working in a nice, clean office, I found myself working as a cashier at a food court restaurant. My life was miserable, and I felt the physical and emotional pain of standing on my feet taking people's money for eight to ten hours a day. One night when I was about to wrap up for the night, I saw my spiritual teacher pass by the restaurant. I invited him for food and a chance to talk. I told him that buying a restaurant was a mistake and I should never have done it, and he responded by saying, "Which part of feeding hungry people with food makes you feel bad?" I had never thought of the services from that angle. This new perception kept me going for eight more years with added energy and enthusiasm.

3

Invite & Accept Change

Everything in our world is changing around us. The environment changes, the people around us change, we change, our wants and needs change. Anticipating and embracing change will keep us aligned with our inner desires. Conscious change is the solution to an unfulfilling and unhappy life.

However, because change will take us to an unknown territory, we are always afraid of it. Change will take us out of our comfort zone and at the same time we are afraid of loss, rejection, failure, criticism, being vulnerable and being judged by other people. We are fearful of making mistakes, of having guilt or the rejection of our loved ones, and this is a legitimate reason for being stuck and continuing our unhappy life.

Conscious change will happen only on one condition, and that is our desire. Many want to change. They talk about change, but talking about it does not and will not help us. Change will happen whether we like it or not. But, rather than reacting to change as an ignorant individual, we can anticipate the change and embrace it. Some changes are good, and some changes will challenge us to create new opportunities. However, if we continue to resist change and stay with our old beliefs, we will suffer.

My husband and I were operating in a 4,000-square-foot warehouse dealing with container loads of imported general merchandise when we were hit with the 2008 economic downturn. Before losing everything, we adapted to change and decided to liquidate our warehouse merchandise and start over with one part of our existing business: custom framing, which we continue to do today. Change is good and necessary to grow and learn. Whether right or wrong, good or bad, it offers great lessons to move forward with confidence.

Routine and doing the same thing over time gets very boring. Our imagination is built to dream, invent and create. When one chapter closes, the next one starts. This is how we always have something to look forward to.

4

LET GO OF THE EGO

Living with the cloud of our ego is a common reason for being unhappy. We are afraid of losing or damaging the identity or the reputation that we have created for ourselves and are stuck there. We only pray for a miracle to happen and take us out of our unhappy life. We can't leave our current life, and starting a new identity looks scary. So, our false ego is blocking us from creating a new life that is authentic and real.

Who do we think we are? Being a human means accepting that we are smaller than a tiny speck of dust in the universe, with a very short life span. What can we do in this time to make any difference anyhow? Not much! Think of ourselves as a fully dependent person who makes mistakes; who is curious; whose heart is full of love, laughter, forgiveness and gratitude. In this case, we don't have an ego to exclude ourselves because of our identity, gender, color of skin, roots, language or ethnicity. We are all human beings, with exactly the same capabilities and vulnerabilities.

What we look like, where we came from, how much money we have, what our job title is, what size house we live in, and what our gender is, in the big picture of life, is nothing to be proud of. Not getting intimidated when we see a celebrity or someone rich, and not getting stuck up and ignorant when we see a poor person with less privileges will keep our ego in balance.

We'll find that the most valuable things in our life are the experiences that we create for ourselves and others; it's the love and support that we give to ourselves and others; it's the service that we offer. It's the love that we share, it's the hand that we give, and it's the feeling that we exude.

What has helped me in the process is that I see everyone as equal that has a need to breathe, eat and go to the bathroom. So, there's no need to feel either superior or inferior to anyone on this planet.

Enlightened individuals know that this life is short, temporary and very unpredictable. What we have today might not be ours tomorrow, and what we don't have today might be ours the next day. Wise people always know this and practice humility.

Ego gives us the mentality of fake pride and a fight for something that is not worth much. Pride of country, culture, language, religion, or anything, for that matter, removes us from our natural state of being. If we accept the Earth as our shared land, borders do not mean anything. If we accept our pride of humanity, we will never volunteer to fight to protect our borders from the enemy with force. If we understand that all the creatures of this world are created equally, we will never kill or be killed for our religious beliefs. These are all tactics used to gain or maintain power.

Our current state of mind is the result of our past thoughts and behaviors that came with our logic and reasoning. We thought these things would make us happy, but they did not. So, if we want change, we will need to isolate ourselves from our normal thoughts, behaviors and actions. We'll need to have the courage to stand up against our normal outer self and bring out the real, authentic self. Believe that with a new set of thoughts, behaviors and actions, our mind can be reset to what we truly desire in our life. Therefore, it is important that we think, do and feel different from our previous self if we want to move away from our self-centered ego. Our new behavior will raise some questions from the people close to us, but this is our internal journey that others may or may not understand. What's important is to remember that this change is necessary for achieving happiness from within.

5

PRACTICE GRATEFULNESS

Gratefulness is activity of the heart. This practice will help us in countless ways to improve our physical and emotional well-being.

Gratefulness fills the heart with joy and makes the world a warm, safe, and supportive place. It also takes our attention off of our self-centered ego to what is outside of us that supports our life. Every time we lose hope or feel down, we can count our blessings at that moment. If we practice gratefulness at least once every day, our life will be transformed at all levels.

As mentioned earlier, nothing in this world is permanent. Everything is in a state of constant change. Knowing that there are so many people who are less privileged than we are living on this earth makes us grateful for what we have, and we will always find less privileged people than ourselves.

Gratefulness is a state of mind that does not depend on what we have outside of ourselves. It is what we have within us that supports our life. It is our breath, it's our body, it's our thoughts, it's our trust, and it's our dependence and connectedness to others and to our environment. Once we go within ourselves, we have a countless number of things that we can be thankful for. This feeling automatically puts us in a safer and happier state of mind. It will take us out of our limited views and show us what we already have.

During one of my deep meditation sessions I opened my eyes and saw something that I had never seen before. I was sitting on the beach, the ocean was still, the birds were singing, the sun was shining through a bunch of trees, and sparing patches of grass were visible among piles of dry, smooth white sand. At that moment, I saw that every little piece of sand, grass, the birds, the trees, the ocean, the clouds, the blue sky, the wind, the bees, and the ants are supporting my life as if they are keeping me in a bubble, protected and safe. I felt enormous gratitude for everything visible and invisible around me. After that experience, there has not been a single moment that I am not thankful for something in my life.

6

TAKE RESPONSIBILITY

The desire to achieve inner peace and happiness depends on the level of our awareness, our maturity and our curiosity, not on our age. Some people will never take responsibility for designing or creating their own actions, and some lucky ones start early in life. Here's the difference: a proactive life versus a reactive life. The ones who are proactive enjoy a more satisfying life, but the ones who are reactive are at the mercy of destiny. They wait until the last minute, until their life crumbles under their feet, and then make some minor adjustments, if any. But in contrast, the proactive people are aware of what they want and which path they are choosing.

To be totally honest, I have seen very ignorant and happy people, but have never seen a miserable proactive individual because the nature of the proactive life is to try new things and make life exciting and challenging. Even if these people fail,

28

they don't seem to be miserable. They get up and start again. Therefore, at any age or stage of life that we are in, we are in the right place to start enjoying the good, the bad and even the ugly for the rest of this journey that is called life.

It's very easy to blame other people and events for our misfortunes. To some extent our past and our childhood experiences do shape our future, but as soon as we are adults and can decide for ourselves, that is the end of this painful life chapter. As adults we can start from where we are and create the rest of our life, rather than feeling sorry for ourselves and blaming others for our problems.

I made my life decisions knowing that they might not be the perfect ones, but they were made according to what I desired most. Almost always, I gave my family and my relationships priority over my career. Very occasionally, I've regretted some of my decisions, but since they are decisions I made knowing all that I knew at the time, I don't blame anyone else for how my life has turned out. This is the beauty of a proactive life.

7

LEAD WITH OUR HEART

Leading with our heart may sound illogical, but it's a wonderful experience if we give it a chance. All our life we have been instructed to use our intellect to make decisions and to learn the ropes of climbing above. We learned from our parents and from school that knowledge is everything, that we can get to the heights of success with our knowledge, but they never thought about the feelings of emptiness we'd experience once we found that imaginary success. Some of us are so buried under the pressure of our daily life that it's impossible to hear our heart beat, let alone take the time to listen to the subtle pull toward what it's attracted to. Most of us live fully submerged in a pool of responsibilities, boundaries, righteousness and identity that make it hard to let go of our logic and what we have built so far, and start to make decisions some other way. We are afraid, unhappy and unsatisfied despite having everything that we thought would make us happy not too long ago. Therefore, we feel there's more—more than what we are and what we long for right now. We are capable of more, and our heart knows that if we fully trust it and go with it, we'll enjoy the ride of life for as long as we have on earth.

We need to do things differently, slowly but surely, and start with ourselves. Take a good look at ourselves in the mirror and look into our own eyes. Are we happy? If not, why not? Try to go beyond our logical, obvious reasons, like "she disappoints me," "he did this," or "I look fat." What do we want to say to ourselves in the mirror? How did we allow her to disappoint us? Or why are we upset over his actions, and what have we done to gain weight? Ask these questions of ourselves, because it is nobody's business to make us unhappy. It's our own mind that does not let us see past it, through our heart to see what is truly there.

We deserve to be happy and find a way to communicate with our heart. Therefore, we must take a moment to look ourselves in the eye every day, and remember to listen to our heart all day long, hearing what it tell us about what it wants us to do.

Here are some examples of dialog between my heart and mind:

My heart tells me to go for a walk every day, but my mind says it's too cold. My heart tells me to call our friend, but my mind says that I'll wait for her call. My heart says to take a break, but my mind says that I must finish this pile of work. My heart says I must help this person, but my mind says that we don't have enough money.

All of us deal with at least a hundred of these situations every day. The next time let's remember to ignore what our mind says and do what our heart says. We might see some temporary setbacks from our usual habits and productivity, but it pays off in the long run.

Heart versus mind at work: We work to offer a service or to produce a product. In most cases, we are one in a pool of people working in a company for one reason: to offer a service or a product. Sometimes, we get distracted by losing the chain of how our service is helping others in the process. When we go to work, ask ourselves, are we proud to be part of this team and the process? Do we know the real benefit that our work gives to the end user? Our answer may be something like, "Yes, I like the team, but the process sucks"; or "Yes, I like the company, but the people suck," or "I hate what I am doing there," and very occasionally we answer, "I love my job and the people that I work with."

We spend more than half of our time at our place of work, doing our job. In addition to providing a service, we have to deal with strangers that either work for us or use our services and products. We face challenges, demands, and upsets that make work a highly stressed place. But only the unaware allow work stress to enter their system and cause physical and emotional damage. You won't lose anything but the stress, if you just do as your heart says. Although our heart-centered behavior benefits the company greatly, we'll gain more by being satisfied by our contribution.

Our heart says, do the right job, but our mind says, I'm not getting paid enough; our heart says to solve this problem, but our mind says it's not our job; our heart says to back up our coworker, but our mind says we can't trust him; our heart says to finish the job at hand, but our mind says, don't work overtime. We must try to put our heart into our work and use it with our coworkers, bosses and clients, because everyone knows when we genuinely take the initiative to solve a problem wholeheartedly.

The same concept can be used with our relationships. We have learned to calculate the balance of give and take even with our loved ones, and occasionally, we get caught up with our own beliefs and rules. We want to offer unconditional love to our kids and our spouse, but we act very cautious in fear of spoiling them or showing our own vulnerability and being taken advantage of. This is not what our heart says about them, however. Our heart says to love them, spoil them and give them as much as we can without any expectations and without causing harm or suffering to ourselves. If we get satisfaction for being of service, or serving our loved ones today, and if we love them unconditionally, this will not change in the future even if we become separated or our egoistic mind tries to manipulate our actions towards them. We never hurt or cause any harm to our loved ones intentionally. All actions against our loved ones are coming from the mind level, not from the heart.

8

MEDITATE

Some of us might not realize the extent of our mind's busyness. Naturally, it runs for twenty-four hours. The recent unverified number that I could find online is that, on average, we have about 70,000 thoughts per day; that is about 4,000 thoughts per hour, and 70 thoughts per minute. I am not sure how accurate it is, but I'm sure that it's close. We don't even know when one thought starts and the other stops; one thought often interferes with the other, and then we go back and forth with the chain of our thoughts. Sometimes we are even too busy with our mind's dialogue that we forget what we are doing at the present moment.

Of course, we are curious creatures and our mind runs wild, especially when we are curious. We ask questions and answer them; we play through good and bad scenarios in our mind. Some of our ideas start to shape in our thoughts and die there soon after.

We have placed a very high value on what we think. Originally, the idea was that if we can think, we can create, and that is completely true. We have created this life with the power of our thoughts. However, there's one missing ingredient: the feeling of satisfaction. We neglected to include the power of our soul, our consciousness, in the equation. This is the reason that after fulfilling all our dreams and desires we are still empty and longing for more, or for something different.

We all know very well that most of our mind's activity does not serve any purpose in our reality. Reality is always different from what we think about. Therefore, quieting the noise in our mind is a necessary step to give the space and time for our heart, or core desire, to come into play and start to communicate with us. This is how we know ourselves and our real inner power to move on in life with clarity and purpose.

Regular meditation will help us to be vulnerable, dependent, grateful and humble in the big picture of life. Meditation will help us to focus on our strengths and let go of everything that doesn't support our life and our purpose. Meditation will help us to be satisfied with who we are and accept ourselves as perfect, with all the imperfections that we think we have. Meditation will help us to listen more and be more attentive to others. Meditation will help us forgive ourselves and others for their mistakes. Meditation will help us get clear on how to live and how we will be remembered once we have passed on.

Meditation is not a religious practice. Although there are set guidelines to follow, its purpose is to quiet our mind. If we think of meditation as the most pleasurable moment of our day that stops us from thinking and stressing, it really doesn't matter what kind of name we give to this practice. If meditation and yoga sound to you like just another daunting task that you must do during the day, you are not alone. One of the reasons many of us don't meditate is because we think we don't have time and that we have more important things to do. However, when we are listening to our favorite song while walking and thinking about nothing else; when we are working on our garden and enjoy touching the soil and the plants, thinking about nothing else; and when we are having passionate sex with our loving partner that takes us out of this world, these are all forms of meditation in action. In this way, we could be meditating throughout the entire day without scheduling a specific time slot for our meditation session.

Furthermore, fasting our seat belt while driving is a task, brushing our teeth is a task, and throwing our garbage out is a task, but we do these things as part of our normal daily activities now. By practicing small but consistent acts of meditation, it becomes part of our routine in no time.

There are those spiritually enlightened individuals who sit silently for hours or days with closed eyes away from the crowds, but there are also those who live among us with open eyes enjoying every second of this life with what they do, see, hear, touch, and taste. What we do is irrelevant; how we do it with pleasure is more important.

If we think we can't sit still for a few minutes to connect with our soul or consciousness, then instead we can do more of those activities that stop us from thinking and put us in the present moment. This is a great starting point for our spiritual journey.

When we are faced with too many choices and the power of our imagination gives us unlimited options, we run circles in our mind. As a result, as Jaggi Vasudev (Sadhguru), one of India's most influential mystics of our time, says, "We got a diarrhea of the mind." The way to cure it is to take control and ask all those noises to stop. We sit still and ask our thoughts to stop the play. In the meantime, we take our breath, which is our life force, into our body with intention and release it back to nature with intention.

If we can stop our mind in the middle of our work, or at any other time, and bring our focus with intentional breathing to now, we have used one of our meditation techniques to be present now, no matter what is going on around you.

9

SPEND TIME IN NATURE & TRAVEL

When we are in nature, we are most connected to our happy place. Whether it is the beach, the mountains, different seasons, parks, gardens, hikes, waterfalls, woods or anywhere that your heart feels at home, that is the place where we can focus, make decisions, think, be ourselves and get charged. By spending more time in nature, we become aware of the Earth's movements, notice the perfection of the system, and get lost in the beauty that is around us. In nature, our body, mind and spirit are aligned.

When we stay in one place, we grow accustomed to the place, the people, and know everything about the place. It becomes our comfort zone where we feel supported and right at home. When we leave this comfort of a known place and people, we find ourselves alone and isolated, and it's a challenge to find our way and get the things that we need.

We'll find that the needs and wants of people everywhere in the world are the same. The same things make them happy and the same things make them upset. We'll know that although we don't know anyone, we'll find people to help us in any way they can. We'll know how to adapt to situations and focus on one thing with one goal at the same time. We'll learn what are the most important things to us and to value them anywhere we are in the world. We'll learn humility and learn to live with less.

Solo trips take the worries of the future out of our mind, so we can focus on now and how to get around. This is when we find peace away from our everyday responsibilities and look forward to exploring and staying in the moment for as long as we can. Spending time in nature separates us from the tension of our everyday life and naturally quiets our mind.

Living on the island of Maui was a life-changing move for me. I had never felt this close to the sunrise, sunset, ocean wave patterns, and wind routes. It helped me understand that we are human Beings, not human Doings. It helped me understand that love, gratitude and humbleness are more valuable than my bank account and my self-centered fake needs. I learned to trust strangers and feel the pain and challenges of being away from my comfort zone, while at the same time feeling blessed to be able to live in a tropical climate in the middle of the Pacific Ocean. Maui has a rainforest jungle, high mountaintops, dry cactus plants, black and dead lava, and an all-around pristine oceanfront and beaches that make it the best spot for achieving higher spirituality.

10

Eliminate Distractions

Our mind is too busy naturally and we care about too many unnecessary things. To free up more time to enjoy life and to have peace of mind, we can declutter our mind and our daily activities. We need to focus on what we want to do, our hobbies, our most important relationships, and how to expand our knowledge and experiences.

If watching television shows, following the news, obsessing over a sports team, stressing about what happened on the other side of the world or who did what gossip, spending time on social media and the phone, playing cards with friends, and being stuck in traffic jams were cut out of our daily schedule, there would be plenty of time for us to enjoy life. Find out what is not important and does not support our life and our goals in life and let go of it. We'll find more time, energy, and focus throughout our day and enjoy our life even more.

This behavior shift will make it possible for us to focus on a few important things rather than caring about too many projects, events or people. As human beings, our time is limited, and we have a limited physical capacity. Every twenty-four hours must be filled with peace, productivity, harmony and zest for living that we can't wait for the next day to begin after each resting period.

Unless we are directly working with these industries, we can live without knowing anything about entertainment news, sports games, politics, violence, reality shows, talk shows, celebrity gossip shows and magazines. We will experience happiness once we stop consuming and start creating. Create a drawing, paint a painting, knit a sweater, bake cookies, learn gourmet cooking or juice mixing, concoct herbal remedies or take up sewing, and share our knowledge.

For the first three months of our move to Maui, we did not have a TV. Just by not spending any time watching TV, both of us were able to work on creative projects that we always wanted to do. My husband started painting, and I started writing and making mandalas.

11

BE EASY

Seriousness in life comes from the rules that we either make for ourselves or we are told to follow. Of course, following rules is always good, but if we always follow rules or try to enforce any rules on others, we limit our imagination, creativity and boundaries. Sometimes, we feel like we need to break most of the unwritten imaginary rules to feel alive.

We can be happy with ourselves, but one of the most precious things in this life is to have someone or some people to enjoy life with. We get our greatest rewards and greatest suffering from the people we love. They can be our strength and our weakness at the same time.

However, life is short and the unexpected often happens. We already understand that we will not be able to change anyone for any reason; we'll need to accept our family for who they are and will need to let go of some people that we don't enjoy. But the most important person in any relationship that we will have is ourselves. We'll need to be understanding, supportive and kind towards others because this is the only thing we have control over and we deserve to receive all of these things from others.

Relationships consist of a give-and-take balance, but enlightened people always give more because they live in abundance and are not fearful of the consequences. They share their love and support with no conditions or expectations.

We design our world our way, and that's the best way to satisfy our soul and carry out our purpose in life. Just remember to breathe and let others breathe at the same time. Be easy and flexible.

So, if we like to live a blissed life, fill it with actions that we enjoy. Surround ourselves with people that we enjoy, and always have something to look forward to.

12

BE PRESENT NOW

We are always in pursuit of happiness rather than experiencing the joy of the present moment. I am not talking about long-term goals or plans, but I am talking about our daily life. Here's how most people go about their typical day: they wake up to do something, dress up to go somewhere, take the car from point a to point b, get coffee on the way, arrive, wait there, most likely accomplish something for a future date, get a quick lunch from a drive-thru chain, need to drop off dry cleaning and run a few other errands, pick up a few things from the grocery store, get stuck in traffic, come home tired, clean up the house and kitchen, prepare dinner, watch TV and fall asleep.

This is an example of a spiritually awakened, mindful individual going about her day: she wakes up; smiles; smells the sheets; feels the touch points of the bed on the body; yawns and stretches;

checks her mood for what to wear for the day; checks the color, comfort and fit of the clothes and how they make her feel; looks in the mirror; walks outside, feels the weather and guesses if it's a hot or cold day but is prepared for both just in case; looks at the sky and sees the clouds; hears the birds; sits in her clean car and adjusts the mirrors and her seatbelt; makes sure she hasn't forgotten anything at home; with pleasure starts the car; sings a song or listens to a podcast; gets there and notices everything: colors, textures, shapes, buildings, trees, flowers, walkways, sounds and smells; waits there while reading her book; smiles and engages in conversations; accomplishes a task for a future date; drives a few blocks farther to stop at a health food store; feels good walking in observing the sights and sounds; gets her quick lunch and sits down to eat while tasting each bite; feels grateful for her meal and for the people who prepared the meal; drops off her dry cleaning and runs her errands; picks up a few things from the grocery store; gets stuck in traffic and starts to sing along with her favorite singer, looking forward to going home; thinks about her colorful dinner plate on the table to surprise her family; comes home, lights some candles, plays background music and starts cooking with passion; and plays a family game before going to bed.

It looks like the spiritually awakened person does more, and perhaps that is why you might think that you don't have the time or patience to do all that. However, the fact is that life is not a destination or a goal that you accomplish, but instead it is a journey to be felt with every minute of your time.

Living in the past or the future takes us away from this moment. Everything that we want to create, experience and accomplish happens right now. If we are busy with our past experiences or dreaming of something that has not happened yet, we will not be able to enjoy the moment.

This moment contains the power to make decisions and execute ideas. If this moment is gone, it's gone forever. Lost opportunities will not come back again. This moment is the only time that we can choose to have joy and spend it with peace, whatever it is that we are doing or wherever that we are. Make the best of our moment by being thankful, optimistic, and a positive thinker.

If we are rushing through our day and activities, we will accomplish our tasks, but we won't remember the journey. If life is a journey, it is made of moments; what we do with these moments and how we remember them makes life blissful and a worthwhile journey.

We don't need to fill every minute of our day. With the amount of stress that we all have, the less we do, the more beneficial it is for our health and happiness.

13

LET GO OF FAKE DESIRES

There are times that we think, if we have this, we'll be happy; if we have that, we'll be set. Or, we tell ourselves that we only have three more years of hard work before we can take time off and enjoy what we have. If our desires are personal wealth and success, I honestly don't know what it means because financial success does not have a set value and it means different things to different people. Have we defined our success level? Is it a house or a big house? Is it a car that we can use to move around, or a luxury sports car? Is it a few pairs of pants and shoes, or a full closet of pants and shoes? We'll need to make that determination before we decide to spend our most valuable time working for our fake desires that not only do not make us happy, but add more options, and more stress to our life.

We must accept ourselves as who we are and be happy with our color, shape and everything that we come with. We are perfect, and we each have a unique gift to offer. It really means nothing what the rest of the world thinks about us or how they perceive us if we continue to be ourselves. There are some people that love us and want to see us happy in our life, like our parents, our children, our supporting spouse, and some of our best friends, and the rest of the world couldn't care less about who we want to become, what we want to do or how we are living our life.

Let go of fake desires, but don't lose our true dreams of growth and the expansion of what our heart desires. Our true desires are the ones that will take us to a happy place; they will give us courage to move on without fear and without looking back. Our true desires are not material, money or fame, but are things that change the quality of our life and the lives of others. They are the ones that contribute to the wellbeing of humanity and the planet. What counts at the end of life is the happy moments when we experienced joy within ourselves and with our loved ones, and the joy of providing the services that satisfy our soul.

14

CHALLENGE FEARS & SELF DOUBT

Once we are aware of our mind's activity and have the control to turn it off when we want to, it is the perfect time to sort out our thoughts that bring us negative emotions. Negative emotions are not to be eliminated from our life, but to be recognized, acknowledged and accepted. We already know that life is composed of both positive and negative emotions. Positive is pleasure and negative is suffering; positive is empowering, while negative is debilitating.

The nature of our being is to be and not to make meanings of things that happen in our lives, but this is not the case. We give meaning, good or bad, to events and experiences of our lives. Sometimes, we mistakenly judge positive events as negative and vice versa. This is all our mind's game. This judgement is based on our imagination, our past experiences and our future expectations.

However, we know that the law of attraction is at work and our mind doesn't know what is real and what is not; it just brings more of what we think to our life. For this reason, negative thoughts and negative emotions need to be identified at the thought level and be recognized and released. Yes, they are part of our lives and we won't be able to eliminate them from our thoughts, but we can be aware the moment such thoughts appear in our mind and be able to release them. This will make the suffering period shorter and shorter, and help us quickly return to our natural state of being, happy and content, no matter what is going on around us.

Fear is the most common negative emotion and probably the biggest. Almost all our decisions are based in fear or love. Fear is mostly the result of our logic and reasoning that our mind suggests, and love is the things that our heart desires.

We are brought up with fear front and center in our life. This is what we were told almost every day by our parents, our teachers and our society—to be careful and to be afraid of the unknown. How many times have we heard the words 'be careful'? What that means is that I'm afraid for our safety and well-being.

When we quiet our mind, meaning we put aside all the dialogue of our mind, we'll hear the voice that comes from our heart. Our heart wants us to be genuinely happy; it wants us to love and to trust. We've heard this inner voice from time to time but haven't paid attention as our logical mind takes over almost immediately. We dismiss the idea that our heart suggests, and we carry on in a world full of fear.

Fear is our body's natural mechanism for warning us about danger. If the danger is real, our life depends on it, but most of the time, the danger is imaginary and has not happened yet, or it is rooted in a negative experience that we had in the past.

We must become aware of our fear in our thoughts, recognize it and acknowledge it. Then, we can respond by consciously asking the fear to leave our thoughts because it is not real. We take some risks by forfeiting fear out of our lives, but that's what makes our life challenging and interesting.

The other common negative emotion that cripples us is self-doubt. Sometimes we hear criticism from other people that makes us upset and sometimes it becomes a turning point in our life. Or, at least, we ignore the criticism by dismissing and not believing it altogether. However, when we doubt ourselves, there's nothing that we can do because we've already listened to the criticism and believed it to be true. Self-doubt causes us to feel inferior and unworthy. It will make us stay quiet when we want to scream.

Self-doubt is another form of fear. It is the fear of rejection, failure, acceptance, criticism, being judged, or laughter. We already know that these kinds of fear are imaginary, and it keeps us from living with love.

We'll have to believe that we are born in a perfect condition. We have something that others don't have. After all, we each have unique DNA that nobody else in the world has. We are good at something that doesn't come to others naturally.

The next time self-doubt appears in our thoughts, we need to double-check it. We must believe in ourselves and be clear on our purpose. Accept ourselves for who we are and be happy with our uniqueness. We need to stay persistent and show confidence despite having fear and self-doubt by acknowledging our strengths and weaknesses, laughing at ourselves and our ideas, admitting our mistakes and moving on, because everyone is exactly the same as we are.

15

Maintain Our Good Health

This ancient Persian expression gives us the real value of health: "Good health is more than having the kingdom." That's how much having good health means. Unfortunately, we know the value of our health when we get sick. Sometimes we go on as if nothing will happen to us, as if we are immune to being sick and vulnerable, but that is not the case. We all are very vulnerable beings that can get sick at any time. However, there are things that science and technology have proven to help with disease prevention and longevity.

Good, real food fuels the body. We are evolutionary, biological creatures. The nature, the Earth, provides for all our needs. However, with the advancement in civilization, our food has been altered from its original nature. Along with that, we are too busy to pay attention to what we are eating. Processed and manufactured food has overtaken almost all our supermarkets. Even the fresh meat and vegetables are compromised with chemicals. With the current lifestyle, our choice is very limited in terms of what we can put in our body as nutritious food.

Obesity, cancer, depression, strokes, heart attacks, and high blood pressure are the major causes of disease and ailments that take away lives. These are very common diseases of our time and major factors for physical, emotional, social, and financial stress and unhappiness. The good news is that if we are aware of how important food is in our lives, we will take responsibility for our own sourcing and cooking of fresh and healthy meals for our own and our family's well-being.

Sleep is as important as food. It's our body's way to rejuvenate and give us a chance to start a new day with a new beginning. When we are young, we don't notice our sleep deprivation as much, but as time goes on, we feel the lack of sleep in our energy and focus level during the day. Obviously, everyone's need for sleep is different, but we all should go with our biological clock and our personal need to get enough rejuvenation time to not jeopardize our full body functioning capacity for the next twenty-four to forty-eight hours.

The other major contributor to our health is movement. We are designed to move. Our joints, muscles, nervous system, skin and mind requires air—oxygen—to function properly consistently. If longevity is on our mind, then it goes hand-in-hand with our lifestyle that consists of good nutritious food, enough sleep and plenty of movement every day.

The other factors that help our health and emotions are sunlight, nature, aromatherapy, music, fresh air, a clean and organized living space, optimism, and good company.

16

ACCEPT UNFORTUNATE EVENTS

Normal life for everyone includes ups and downs. Sometimes, we feel like we are on top of the world; we feel proud, successful, and unbreakable. But there are times that we feel sad, heartbroken, defeated and hopeless. When we understand that the down times are also part of normal life, it's much easier to accept those unhappy moments and go through them with patience and integrity.

When we lose our job, when we lose our loved ones, when we divorce our spouse, or when we are unhealthy, we need to understand that this too shall pass. Time will heal most of our physical and emotional wounds, but if we can accept them quickly, the process is much shorter and less painful.

One thing to remember is that we are not in control of many things in our lives. We never know what might happen the next moment or the next day. This is the biggest reason to not take ourselves too seriously and falsely blame ourselves for some of our misfortunes. Whether this misfortune has happened because of our own negligence or wrong decision or someone else's hands were involved is irrelevant. The damage has been done and there's no point in going backward.

We always accept the painful events and situations as they are meant to happen, and with a little change in our own perception, we can decide to let go of the worries, grudges, fears and hopelessness of the moment. Happy people find something positive in every negative situation and go through it with grace, knowing that everything in life is transient. Have the best expectations for what is to come because we will start from a stronger position after each downturn.

17

FIND OUR TRIBE & VIBE

We all have our own specific characteristics that might not get along with everyone. We need to socialize and to trust a few good friends in life and at work to give us a sense of belonging. It's a group of people that being around them gives us comfort. We feel understood. We share our happiness and sadness with these people, and these people are always available to listen to us without judgement. It is as if they know us more than our parents or siblings, although our tribe can include our parents, siblings and family members.

Our tribe might be one, two, three or ten people that protect us. We can count on them to have our back when necessary and we do the same for them. People who have close friendships and spend time and energy with their tribes are the happiest.

Engaging with our tribe is important. Sometimes we just feel better in their presence; however, if we like to take the comfort a step further, try to engage with them in fun activities. Not only do we enjoy the moment with pleasure, but we also create fun memories for ourselves that we can recall at any time in the future.

Spending time with our tribe is our happy social time, but when they are not around, we need to be happy with ourselves. Something that will help us stay away from worries and negative thoughts is to be engaged in a hobby. Hobbies represent the creative side of our life and preoccupy us with our imagination. Choose a hobby that you enjoy. This is an activity for yourself and how you express your passion for life. Whether it's painting, writing, music, sports activity, knitting or jam making, it's vital that we submerge ourselves with our creativity because this can become our medicine for loneliness, depression and body aches.

18

LIVE WITH LESS

When we are happy and content with ourselves and our life, we don't seem to mind the things we are lacking. Instead, we find a way to work with the things we have. The desire to have more comes from immaturity and insecurity. The other reason is that we compete with visible or sometimes invisible people in our mind. We want to be the greatest by having great things, and we work hard to have those great things. Sometimes, we take our health, our loved ones, and our life for granted in pursuit of acquiring great things. Yes, great things might put our name on the list of famous and successful people, but they'll never give us the peace of mind that as a human being we crave.

It is unfortunate that many of us realize the value of life and time too late. Our bigger house, our bigger car and our bigger diamond ring will take our time, energy and attention away from experiencing true joy in our life. These all will bring temporary happiness to us, and as we know, everything around us is in constant change. Our house needs upkeeping; stuff to fill it with and to maintain; our car needs constant maintenance; our diamond jewelry needs a safe and two locks every time we leave the house. The more keys we have, the more stress we have. With those keys and that stuff comes responsibility and a level of fear for protecting them. When we think of it at the end, it doesn't make sense to acquire any more than what meets our basic needs.

Organization and cleanliness make our life easier and happier. Regular house cleaning, office cleaning, closet cleaning, drawer cleaning, and table cleaning puts us in a higher, happier state of mind. Not only does it offer health benefits, it also helps us to concentrate well on our tasks and most valued relationships.

If we can have less greed, less friends, less keys, less stuff, less distractions, less gossip, less thinking, less news, less social media, and less consumption, our life will become happier. This is when we concentrate on our life rather than our life in relations with others.

19

NEVER COMPARE OURSELVES TO OTHERS

It is human nature to feel jealous sometimes when we see that our classmates are reaching a higher position than we are, or are making more money, or have found love before us, but the truth is that we add to our sadness when we compare ourselves to others and see the lack of things in our life. That is a cause for disappointment and resentment. Happy people always see where they are in life compared to what kinds of decisions they have made in the past. Sometimes those decisions are not the correct ones, and sometimes we don't know what the correct decision might have been. Life is so fluid and ever-changing that we choose one way and we can never know what would have happened if we chose the other way.

Anyhow, we are here because of our past decisions, life events, experiences, knowledge, connections, skills and luck. Everything does not happen the way we want it to. Even when we think with a little bit of jealousy, we can think back on all the good things that we have and be content with them. Life is not a race and it is not a destination. It is a journey that each one of us individually takes and are responsible for. Nobody in this world has the unique gifts that we have, and nobody in this world was in the same position, with the same upbringing, same place and same imagination as we possess.

What we do in our life is entirely up to us. We might be able to invite luck to ourselves by being at the right time and doing the right thing, but we still can't know if today's luck will bring us misery tomorrow. Therefore, comparing ourselves with others is a waste of time, and an unnecessary race to nowhere that keeps us ignorant of why we were born in the first place.

We are one; our mission and goal is one, and it's only our responsibility and our decision about how we spend our life all by ourselves without regard to others. The only purpose of other people in our life is to help us carry out our goals and imaginations while we do the same for them, but we will always be the priority on our list.

20

LOVE OURSELVES

There's another famous Persian expression that says, "When I am alive, the world is alive," meaning the world is alive while I am living. Otherwise, we are history. We only have our breathing body to go through life and experience this wonderful journey. So, it should take priority.

What we do while we are alive is very important to live, and that happens when we love ourselves, our physical body, our shape, our color, our skin, our imperfections, and our personality. If we don't love ourselves, it's up to us to change it. Chances are that we are pretending to be someone we are not, and that is why we are disappointed with ourselves.

We need to give ourselves a chance to grow, to make mistakes, to fail, and to experience loss, loneliness, and sadness. This is how we become wise. Our emotional state might change from morning to afternoon to night, but to know that we are always the priority, we know how to make our decisions and how to behave and what to do. If we are tired, say we are tired and rest; if we need help, ask for it; if we have a weakness, admit it and let it go; if we are challenged with pride of any sort, kill our ego, knowing that we are a human being and we are on a very short journey here on this Earth.

Love ourselves when we lose our job; love ourselves when our relationship breaks; love ourselves when our kids are sick; love ourselves when we are sick; love ourselves when traveling, working, playing or eating. If we can do this with a sense of humbleness and gratitude for our vulnerability, we give the world the gift of a loving person. We might not be able to solve other people's problems, or offer our services, but we will not add any stress or unnecessary negative vibration in our life around our loved ones.

Therefore, when we are alive, we eat what we consider is healthy, we move our body regularly, we rest when we need to, we do our job with passion, and we make life simple and easy for ourselves. It is also very important to know that we are not in control and cannot fix all the world's problems. We were born alone, we will live alone and we will die alone. What we do while we are alive is all up to us. We choose our happiness and stress level; we choose how complicated our life should be; we have control of what to believe and what to ignore. This is the beauty of life.

We can choose our permanent home, the Earth, to be a warm, safe and beautiful place that supports our life, or a cold, dark and dangerous world that takes away our life. It is the power of our imagination. We have the power to say no to things that do not support our life—the processed fast food, the constant need to update our electronics, the unnecessary urge to watch the news, or the time-wasting consumption of what other people do on social media.

When we love ourselves, we give a gift to our family and the world. It's not important where we live and what we do, as long as we make everything work for us with the utmost grace and modesty and live our life moment by moment one day at a time.

About the Author:

Born and raised in Afghanistan, Farima lives on the Hawaiian Islands and enjoys a blissful life. She writes and is a practical practicing yogi on the path to self-discovery and higher spirituality. She gets her inspiration from the teachings of Rumi, the thirteenth-century Persian scholar.

Author of:

- <u>How to Live Your Life with 7 Treasures You Own</u>
- 20 Life Lessons Series
  - o <u>20 Life Lessons For Your 20s</u>
  - o <u>20 Life Lessons For Your 30s</u>
  - o <u>20 Life Lessons For Your 40s</u>

To sign up for FREE Meditation Class for Beginners please visit:

Pursuing Happiness: 20 Life Lessons

www.FarimaJoya.com
farima@farimajoya.com
Message: 510-275-3497
Facebook: @farimawjoya
Twitter: @farimajoya

Much gratitude to you for going through the Pursuing Happiness: 20 Life Lessons to Find Real Happiness.

Please share your thoughts and leave a short comment to let me know what you found useful in this eBook, and how it can be helpful to your life.

www.farimajoya.com/shop/
Pursuing Happiness

Share Your Love